Who is Afraid of Mongo wa Swolenka

A One Act Play

Mbuh Tennu Mbuh

Langaa Research & Publishing CIG
Mankon, Bamenda

Publisher
Langaa RPCIG
Langaa Research & Publishing Common Initiative Group
P.O. Box 902 Mankon
Bamenda
North West Region
Cameroon
Langaagrp@gmail.com
www.langaa-rpcig.net

Distributed in and outside N. America by African Books Collective
orders@africanbookscollective.com
www.africanbookscollective.com

ISBN: 9956-763-89-6

DISCLAIMER
All views expressed in this publication are those of the author and do not
necessarily reflect the views of Langaa RPCIG.

Praise for the Play

"Africa's past and present autocrats, all rolled into one, are here lampooned in the person of His Royal Excellency Bob Gbadarango Binyambutu Buthablaizi aka BGB², Celebrated Leader of Nubialand and Guardian of the Revolution. Steeped in a recognizable political ethic of self-aggrandizement, self-gratification, demagoguery, violence and neo-colonialism, Buthablaizi seeks to maintain his hold on power by fair or foul means. On the other hand are the forces of change, embodied in the exiled Mongo wa Swolenka and his group of home-based genuine intellectuals who must do battle, not only with an evident Gestapo machinery but also with belly-minded turncoats, to restore sanity to the land. In his one act tragi-comedy, *Mongo Wa Swolenka*, Mbuh Tennu Mbuh's satirical project foregrounds the role of the intellectual in society from the Foucaultian premise that where there is power, there will be 'strong' opposition. The playwright's eclecticism, witnessed in the intertextual interstices marrying aspects of African/world history, politics and literature to good effect, beautifully integrates characterization, humorous dialogue, poetry and apt diction in this wake-up call to African tyrants and intellectuals alike."

Eunice Ngongkum, Associate Professor, African Literature, University of Yaounde I

"In this succinct yet intricately imagined and profoundly crafted play, Mbuh has returned to the question of the failed postcolonial state with a fresh breath. The play is an apt dramatization of all what has gone awry in the postcolonial nation. The playwright deftly describes this sorry state of affairs with his neologism "gunocracy" which symbolizes the complete failure of the state apparatus: failed leadership that relies on the argument of the gun to not only impose and maintain itself in power but equally to implement its anti-people policies, failed intellectualism which fails to stand up for and educate the masses but rather opts for betrayal of the popular cause and the argument of self-aggrandizement. This dense yet humorous play is set in Nubialand the representation par excellence of what every black African state has become; caught up as it were in the tragic hold of its unpleasant colonial past, the machinations of a treacherous international system and its own numerous internal tensions."

Professor Blossom Fondo, Associate Professor of Postcolonial Literature, University of Yaounde II, Cameroon

"In *Who's Afraid of Mongo Wa Swolenka?* a book launch is planned which, from information given to His Royal Excellency Gbadarango Binyambutu Buthablaisi, by a traitorous intellectual seeking preferment; and by his security agents, is a campaign led by disgruntled writers and intellectuals of Nubialand for the return of their exiled colleague and international award winner, Professor Mongo Wa Swolenka. How the celebrated leader of Nubialand and master of gunocratic politics responds to the prevailing circumstances is the nerve centre of dialogue, action and morality in the play."

John Nkemngong Nkengasong, Writer and critic, University of Yaounde I, Cameroon

Dramatis Personae

His Excellency: leader of the Kingdom of Nubialand
Colonel Amin: Head of His Excellency's Secret Service
Mariama: His Excellency's Secretary and paramour
Chinwazu Nwapa
Nicodemus Yessah — Intellectuals
Benyala Ba
Dogo: His Excellency's hangman
Officer

The play was first performed in the Amphi 300 of the University of Yaoundé by the Yaoundé University Poetry Club in collaboration with the Yaoundé University Theatre to commemorate the first anniversary of the killing of the Nigerian activist, Ken Saro-Wiwa. That pioneer cast was as follows:

Tita Tabi Emmanuel – *His Excellency*
Rose Ofe – *Mariama*
Stephen Chia Yong – *Professor Yessah*
Willie Mushing – *Benyala Ba*
Richard Tchoutezo – *Colonel Amin*
Tafor Ateh Kmchwang – *Officer/Dogo*

Giddy Brown – *Musical interlude*

Artistic Director – *Tita Tabi Emmanuel*
Assistant – *Kizitus Mpoche*

Scene I

[*Late morning. HIS EXCELLENCY's office, furnished to taste. A life size portrait of his own saintly pose dominates the background. He is singing in a broken harmony, marching*]

HIS EXCELLENCY:

> I remember when I was a soldier!
> Hipi yap yap hipi hipi yap yap,
> I remember…[*pause*]

Nonsense! Absolute shit and nonsense! Prove my credentials because I've allowed leniency to make heroes of spineless dogs? How do you prove your credentials when you lead the blind and the gullible? And especially this bald-headed breed that I am cursed with every bleeding day in this doomed Kingdom with its lackadaisical intellectual attitudes! [*glances at the papers on his table, thoughtful*] Anyway, I'm still the boss and the pilot, the lawgiver and the executioner and should blame no one but my own humanity for such a deadly sin. [*short laugh, then resumes his song*]

> I remember when I was a beggar!
> What a miracle now that I'm a hero!
> I remember Lord I am your servant
> I remember, Papa God I thank you!

O yes, even the Lord is my shepherd, to think of it now, and who deprives me of my room in the mansion, who? How many pay rises do they expect from me within just a single life time? To be so generous as to become a beggar myself is immortal sin number two. One was enough and if they don't like it now, and given the economic nightmare the treasury is going through, then they should seek the frontier before I change my mind...

[gentle tap and the door half opens]

MARIAMA: Professor Yessah, Sir...

HIS EXCELLENCY: *[snappy]* Ah, him and again so late! Is he so thick-skulled, Maria to stretch my patience to breaking point? Let him in! *[MARIAMA withdraws smiling, to himself]* Such lame beggars, lobbying for a place on the Round Table of the winning team when even their superiors don't qualify as reserves!

YESSAH: *[coming in, excited]* My very loyal greetings, Your Excellency!

HIS EXCELLENCY: What do you take me for, Nicodemus Yessah? *[glances at his watch]* What notion of time do you operate by, Professor? My modus operandi, Sir, is GMT, not BMT, and no more, no less!

YESSAH: *[almost prostrating]* My heartfelt apologies, my Excellency! But as long as we remain black, Sir, can we ever substitute black man's time?

HIS EXCELLENCY: That's a simple question of pigmentation, Yessah, not of the mind. *[in self-flattery]* In fact, on my recent trip for check up, the medics were amazed to discover that my IQ is actually seventy-five percent Caucasian, which explains why my policies appeal so much to Western consciousness.

YESSAH: No one doubts that Sir, at least not to me, absolutely. You simply mesmerise them and us all!

HIS EXCELLENCY: And yet, you can still afford to plant me on the same spot for exactly *[another glance at his watch]* thirty-three minutes zero second by my Omega!

YESSAH: Very sorry, my lord, very sorry. I ... I had to make a phone call, and you know the headache with the lines Sir.

HIS EXCELLENCY: [*screaming*] Make a damn phone call, while I, His Royal Excellency Bob Gbadarango Binyambutu Buthablaizi, aka BGB[2], celebrated leader of the Kingdom of Nubialand and Guardian of the People's Revolution, is waiting! ... [*with pain in his voice*] Waiting for you, Yessah!! What's become of you *okro*-soup Professors of no consequence? And mark you, there is absolutely nothing wrong with my phone lines; the problem is your skull that fails to recognise a benevolent messiah when you see one in my humble personality.

YESSAH: I am terribly sorry, Your Excellency.

HIS EXCELLENCY: Go and sorry your mother's *pima*! [*notices* MARIAMA, *coming in with a pile of letters on a tray and clears his throat in confusion*] Hmm, not now Mariama ... bring them in when Professor Yessah leaves.

MARIAMA: Yes, Sir. [*goes out and closes the door after her*]

HIS EXCELLENCY: Now Nicodemus, what is on your mind that you won't let me be for even a second? Out with it!

YESSAH: Er ... may I sit down my Excellency?

HIS EXCELLENCY: Yes, of course, yes. Let it never be said that I'm inhospitable to builders of the Kingdom. [*turns away slightly, toward audience*] Beggarly idiots! [*to* YESSAH] But be fast, I have only fifteen hours twenty-five minutes left for the day, and the sins of millions to sort through!

YESSAH: [*sits down methodically*] Thank you Sir. You see Sir, in this turbulent century officialdom can be a big handicap to personal, collective, and national advancement.

HIS EXCELLENCY: If your mission here is to deliver a lecture on officialdom and advancement, I'll advise you to seek another audience, Professor.

YESSAH: Not at all Your Excellency, not at all! ...You always mistake my ice-breaking approach. You see the fly that never heeds advice follows the corpse...

HIS EXCELLENCY: Look, Nicodemus, I have work to do, if all you bring is a bag of outdated forebodings. Kindly excuse me!

YESSAH: *Haba*! There you go again your Excellency ... mistaking me all over again! A bit of patience Sir! Work will not run away and even then it is not your cross. As a matter of fact, rumour has it that you stretch yourself too much, whereas others are there to do the job for you. [*challenging*] But now that you want to become the proletariat Jesus Christ of the Kingdom, what if I tell you that at this very moment some gentiles are plotting to precipitate your trip to Golgotha?

HIS EXCELLENCY: [*laughs expansively*] Tell me some other yarn, Nicodemus! Precipitate my trip to Golgotha, you say! Who dares, when all they do is whisper behind my back? Toothless bulldogs, eh?

YESSAH: And even then, most dangerous Sir. And their bite may be any time. You can take it or leave it, Sir, I must dare to sound insolent even to my venerable liege. Why should it be otherwise when the planks of the Rubicon creak under our weight, tempting fate? Sir, certain erstwhile loyal citizens are allergic to your existence and style of leadership, period!

HIS EXCELLENCY: [*thoughtful, almost to himself*] Allergic to my leadership and style of existence? How can they, how, when all I do is offer them paradise on earth? [*pours himself a drink; offers one to* YESSAH] Okay Nicodemus, maybe I rush ahead of my shadow once too often, and maybe I should take you seriously some time. [*turns toward audience again, in a fierce whisper*] A horrid clown! [*to* YESSAH, *clings glasses gingerly*] Now, tell me, Nicodemus, who are these over-zealous and God forsaken nihilists?

YESSAH: [*victorious*] Aha! Now you begin to come around Sir. That's why I have been plaguing your royal peace for a whole week now, seeking audience. [*sips*]. May I only remind you now Sir, of the wisdom of our ancestors … one hand washes the other … you eat a black plum when your brother is up in the tree … one hand cannot tie a bundle … a friend in need is a friend indeed … *eheh*, scratch my back, I scratch your back … one good turn, Sir …

HIS EXCELLENCY: [*brutally*] Ha! Blackmailer! I should have been wiser, rather than let myself blink in your presence, green mamba in green grass! Now you're treading on the edge of my patience, Professor!

YESSAH: No your Excellency, not at all! It's not blackmail … Er, I must confess that I've never disguised my ever-ready appreciation for a possible Cabinet … favour, yes … as long as it doesn't impede your royal vision. Yet, a man must ask for his grub Sir, if his stomach groans, and mine is a groaning burden. At least you can't blame me for being self-reliant and self-conscious.

HIS EXCELLENCY: Yes, I know Nicodemus, and still it changes nothing. How on earth can you conceive of a marriage between stage clowning and my Kingdom's strong room or its mental factory, as you so ridiculously phrased in your statement of intent? [*biting his words and preying on* YESSAH] Politics is hard stuff my dear Prof, and not some kindergarten lamentation to friends, Romans, and countrymen.

YESSAH: [*cringes*] *Kai!* You are unfair to me my lord!

HIS EXCELLENCY: And not without good reason, you think? You'll only cause me tons of headaches like your fugitive brother-in-book-slavery, Nstama Diko who has burdened me with destitution here and—for safe sanctuary, I hear—now washes plates in the Queen's kitchen. And you know the boastful plagues I receive from those dollar-demented idiots at Brettonwoods. I hate systemic abortions, Nicodemus, and you'll be no good, I fear, beyond imaginative tomfoolery. I am a man of action, no more, no less!

YESSAH: Okay, forget about my desire, Your Excellency. It's the fate of a faithful servant to receive tongue lashes from the invulnerable master. What can a man do but say his say to his liege and wait for the best? I've said my say, Sir, your ever vigilant servant.

HIS EXCELLENCY: Now Nicodemus, we're not in the Royal Nubian Theatre. Cut out sentiments; they make my belly turn. [*pats him on the shoulder and pours more whiskey into his glass*] But tell me, who're these disgruntled beetles?

YESSAH: [*scratches his head*] My colleagues your Excellency, and most likely with non-intellectual, even diplomatic, back-up.

HIS EXCELLENCY: [*triumphant*] Ekzakly! I knew all along, unblinking prophet that I was born to be, seer beyond the steeled frontiers! Just typical of all clowns and book-slaves! Impish intellectualism, the gross humbug of the millennium, brandishing contrary and contradictory theories, embracing and stabbing each other! Lame Wakiri brain bugs! Akunyams!

YESSAH: [*conspiratorial*] You over simplify the gravity of the situation, your Excellency. They're no clowns and are certainly not clowning. Their minds tick like a clock, and they're alert to every scratchy detail. The group calls itself *Campaigners for the Salvation of Nubialand*. Their first plan of action is to campaign for the return from exile of our colleague, Professor Mongo Wa Swolenka and then …

HIS EXCELLENCY: [*bangs on the table and* YESSAH *staggers in fright*] Never, you hear? Never under my watch! Let them continue to send their blasphemous petitions to every nook and crevice of the universe, whether from wooded Benakuma to some polar blot, or from the Vatican to Pennsylvania Avenue, still I'll not budge, *pima*! Is it not enough that I offer them the leeway to communicate and perceive paradise always on the horizon, whereas elsewhere they'd be excommunicated or executed and fed to the dogs? They're playing with fire, Professor Yessah! [*breathes heavily paves the room*]

YESSAH: People may say things Your Excellency, and they always do, but nobody ever wishes to play with fire.

HIS EXCELLENCY: [*stops suddenly, calmer*] You think so? [*thoughtful*] Still people may say things, you say? But tell me Nicodemus, what are they saying that I don't yet know, and what's really at stake?

YESSAH: [*relieved*] Not much for now, my lord, not really much.

HIS EXCELLENCY: What d'you mean, not much, Nicodemus? Like the straw against a balloon, you know it'll take just a single bullet, Nicodemus, just one, to end my dreams. And what shall the people do without me, their dream-maker and giver?

YESSAH: God forbid, Your Excellency! For now, however, not much that can't be salvaged, Sir. But you must act fast because time is always priceless and the stitch in time may yet save the glow of the crown and the Kingdom.

HIS EXCELLENCY: [*gesticulates*] Trust me, Nicodemus, trust me for fast, accurate action!

YESSAH: [*flattering*] I see you're still the army General you were some five years ago your Excellency ... no change at all! Even advanced democracy can't take away the leopard spots.

HIS EXCELLENCY: And yet, you people still want to dare General Chameleon? Am I not the democratic Maradona of the United Nations who is still subservient to Divine Guidance? I tell you what? I'll Rushdie all of your satanic impulses into your mother's *kabas* before you know what's happening. Ungrateful daemons! And this certainly with all your mercenary collaborators like Britain's Blackmailing Corporation. And that arch-blackmailer, Robbinhood Wyte ... Just wait, I'll Dele Giwa his bones like the Sheriff of old into sawdust for the winds pick up and they'll rattle like a sweet Bikutsi melody ha ha ha, *bebele Zamba*! That'll be a beautiful diversion, Nicodemus, one of those rare past-times in this *ngoundou* headache of leadership. The next time that hairless ape seeks an interview with me, I'll just blast off ... [*mimics a voice*] Hallo ... yes, Mr. Big Mouth Robbinhood Wyte ... here comes your paramour's letter with love from Delilah, ha ha ha!

YESSAH: I beg your Excellency not to be too presumptuous, if I may be so forward myself. They're well organized Sir, and tomorrow's press conference for instance will set things in motion.

HIS EXCELLENCY: [*seems to stumble over his ego; bangs the table again*] A press what?

YESSAH: Conference, your Excellency.

HIS EXCELLENCY: Over my dead body! [*spins round suddenly, grabs YESSAH savagely by the lapels*] A book launch or a press conference you capital fool?

YESSAH: [*shrugs free, nonplussed*] You see, Sir, the book launch is just a camouflage to ensnare your suspicion. I thought I should let your Excellency know this before it's too late and before you get it from a different source.

HIS EXCELLENCY: Then what on earth has that good-for-nothing fool of a Colonel been doing in charge of my SS1? [*grabs the phone and paunches a number, and in a fine-tuned voice, very deliberate*] Colonel Mvog Badmasi Yakubu Amin of terminal onchocerciasis, report here immediately, *Sir*! [*slams down the receiver; to* YESSAH] Now Nicodemus, tell me, shall the American Ambassador still be in attendance? You know that's a bug I've tried to pocket in vain.

YESSAH: Yes, your Excellency. In fact all of NATO, the EU, the Commonwealth, but not the Chinese; I'm not very sure about the Kremlin.

HIS EXCELLENCY: Okay … okay … What 'xakly d'you people plan to tell these diplomatic bugs whose only good is to poke their long snouts where they shouldn't?

YESSAH: I've stated everything here, your Excellency [*opens a folder and hands over clipped papers to* HIS EXCELLENCY] The fruit of patriotic patience and devotion, Sir.

HIS EXCELLENCY: Very good, very, very! [*flips through the pages and reads at random*] Campaign for international solidarity … international boycotts and news blackout … travel bans … overseas bank accounts … tax havens … genocide and its makers in Morooniambutu, Migbalimbutu, Jumbrumambutu, Gogodoshmbutu … [*pauses*] What on earth, in the name of the Holy Mother, have I got to do with these places and their diarrhoeal fates?

YESSAH: The Group is convinced Sir, and will insist to the international community with the aid of what they call evidence, that you consistently manipulate the unrest in these States to personalize the resources through loyal men who only pretend to oppose you, benefit from foreign assistance and humanitarian aid, and finally divert attention from what they call the excesses of your rule so as to eternalise it. They claim to have gathered incontrovertible evidence, your Excellency.

HIS EXCELLENCY: Fools, as if my eternity depends on their opinion! Let them prove only one fact and I'll concede defeat in principle. [*flashing the file in* YESSAH's *face*] This is all intellectual garbage, Nicodemus, as far as political and diplomatic manoeuvrings go, and I'm surprised that there'll be an audience for it.

[*a sharp knock on the door, enter* COLONEL MVOG BADMASI YAKUBU AMIN]

MVOG AMIN: [*stiffens to attention*] 'Morning your Excellency!

HIS EXCELLENCY: What's this I'm getting all over the place, *Mister* Badmasi Yakubu Amin?

AMIN: What your Excellency, if you don't mind?

HIS EXCELLENCY: Your mother's blasted *pima*, that's what, and I do mind *Mister*! [*breathes heavily*] What was the content of your Monday report, Section three sub four to six inclusive?

AMIN: It was about the book launch at the Town Hall, Sir.

HIS EXCELLENCY: What book launch, Colonel numbskull? How did you come by your facts, *Mister*?

AMIN: Well, your Excellency, the Report was the fruit of information gathered through our normal channels …

HIS EXCELLENCY: Holy Mary! Gather you say! Are you in charge of *gathering* information, *Mister* Amin? What then is the fucking use of my Propaganda Service? You can as well go down the Central Market now and gather your information from every illiterate market woman about the book launch of Professor Nso'ika Mazuwiy, you hear? [*in a pathetic voice*] Why do you make me the laughing stock of buy'am-sell'ams, why?

AMIN: I'm sorry about any ill-conceived and unintended eventuality your Excellency.

HIS EXCELLENCY: You think being sorry now will repair the damage to my person? This is intelligence work, *Mister* Colonel, hard nuts to chew and not pea nuts which any toothless fool can munch … You must coordinate *Sir* – yes, coordinate, that's the word – not just *gather* every bit of rubbish that suits your fancy. Have this … [*flings* YESSAH's *papers at* AMIN] Read what is written by one of those you always describe as barren University imps who are good at nothing but demonstrating for a pay rise quarterly.

AMIN: [*gathers the papers*] I am truly sorry your Excellency. It has never happened before now; it will never happen again after this.

HIS EXCELLENCY: I'm truly shocked, Colonel Amin. I thought you were always watching my back so I could sleep with both eyes closed all the time, but now I know better.

AMIN: As I said, Your Excellency, this is a one-off and will never, never repeat itself again.

HIS EXCELLENCY: [*after a brief silence, almost intimate*] Okay … sit down. Listen Badmasi. It's now a crisis situation and a lot, including my future, may depend on the outcome. Whatever you mistook for child's play is now war declared on my person and regime. The book launch is the mask for a press conference whose aim is to smear my regime and topple me.

AMIN: [*clicks his heels together*] Then we arrest them, Your Excellency!

HIS EXCELLENCY: Yes, we can easily arrest them now, and end the humbug, but that'll be giving them an easy defence. The underdog always receives the most sympathy in international conclaves. So we just wait until the last second when they must have scratched out their own shallow graves and then desert-storm their barren arses out, *bam*! I won't relent in consideration, and I must be vindicated.

AMIN: [*timidly*] The last press release from the American Embassy, Sir, alluded to the need for proportionate reaction in any eventuality.

HIS EXCELLENCY: Proportionate my foot! That's total bullshit, you hear! They think we're blind to their real intentions, eh? Their double edge diplomacy of bite and blow; the carrot and the stick; permanent interests, not permanent friends. Swines! But I choose my friends, Amin, and decide whether or not to accept the carrot, which is often a poisoned gift in any case. But I can easily charge their gorillas here of espionage and give my vote every time to Beijing and what'll they say, eh, when the balance again tilts eastward? But I'll spit this into their faces when I next go to New York … I'm no Mallam Hussein with miserable creeks, nor Fidel Castro with a forsaken island. I reign supreme over a whole Continent-Kingdom, not a fingernail island. No one pokes his nose into the privacy of my eagle nest and go free, *pima*!!

YESSAH: [*who has been hitting the bottle behind* HIS EXCELLENCY's *back and is now slightly tipsy*] They may restrain the last stand-by agreement, Sir...

HIS EXCELLENCY: Shu'rup, will you? No one will blackmail me again into capitulation. I still have my timber and ozone chaos is no friend to red skin. But if not of useless constituencies like your Kig'limbutu suburbs and corrupt municipalities like Ednuoambutu, Ajubambutu and Urukusamaymbutu, I'll still be in bed now, and not up already nursing a nagging headache. [*pads him on the shoulder, smiling*] But never mind, Nicodemus … whenever I sniff danger my mind metamorphoses into hyper dynamics of Microsoft wizardry. [*laughs self-indulgently; to* AMIN, *friendly*] Er, B.Y.A. … let me see … any program for tomorrow should be carried forward, but that press conference may go on but MUST NOT take place!

AMIN: [*shoots up, clicks his feet together*] Yes Sir!

HIS EXCELLENCY: Set to work right away...put up strategies, both crude and humanitarian because each card its appropriate turn. In any case... let me see... [*consults papers*] Yes, they are scheduled to start at 5pm. Let them go in and start grumbling...say 45 minutes. Then you descend on them -- *bam*!

AMIN: [*again stiffens*] Yes Sir, you can count on me!

HIS EXCELLENCY: Or else you count your head off, Badamassi. I expect your first briefing this afternoon. Ask Mariama to bring in that file.

AMIN: Yes Sir!! [*goes out*]

HIS EXCELLENCY: Now, Nicodemus, you are to keep me informed of even the slightest move they make...

[*door crashes open*]

MARIAMA: [*furious*] I thought the letters were due after the Professor's departure, *Sir*!

HIS EXCELLENCY: You thought! Who now gives the orders here, you hussy? I alone determine when to give the orders, you hear?

YESSAH: [*staggers in confusion*] Excuse me your Excellency... I'm sure we are through... Good day your Excellency...

HIS EXCELLENCY: Not so fast, Nicodemus... er, keep me informed, yes, of everything. Then after the performance

– if all goes well – call on me again for a sign of my gratitude.

YESSAH: Thank you very much your Excellency. There'll be no hitch, you'll see. Good day! [*staggers out*].

MARIAMA: [*hotly*] Yes, Mr. Holy President of the Universe... I'm really your eternal robot, remote-controlled, shuffled and tossed, as your holy fancy desires... Bring the letters before the Flood...no, bring them after Eternity, when Jesus shall be no more. After all I'm your waste paper basket, your stand-by generator, only useful when the lamps of officialdom have been extinguished. It's humiliating the way you treat me!

HIS EXCELLENCY: No dear, you don't understand me. I couldn't do otherwise and play lover-boy in front of that clown. That'll simply inspire him for ridiculous representations for stage lice. [*amorous*] But come now... let me pinch those stubborn buttocks a bit...

MARIAMA: [*slaps off his hand*] Lay your claws off me, Sir! Yes, I know what follows the usual rehearsals [*mimics*] You see my dear, Empress Josephine will spend two good days sweating up the pyramids to beat the years on her heels while we stay here in paradise. [*in her normal voice*] No way *Sah*! I'm tired of this wait-for-your-chance farce. Why not lock me in a fridge and bring out the inert lump whenever you please? [*coyly*] As if I can't be a better First Lady.

HIS EXCELLENCY: Now Mariama, we have gone over this a hundred times. What you insinuate is simply impossible. We must be oriented by some semblance of decency if only for public consumption and newspaper headlines. But you know you're always my Ihuouma... come on...

MARIAMA: [*a bit soft in tone*] But you also know what I'd rather be. After all Ihuouma will never have the opportunity to scale the pyramids with all the publicity.

HIS EXCELLENCY: Oh, do you mean to say you prefer those barren cones of archaeological rubbish to the sunny and palm beaches of the Bahamas?

MARIAMA: You say so because you don't know a woman's heart and will never know the risks I run. It only suffices for any long nose Immigration Officer to smell the content of your parcels. Then I'll be salvaged to America forever never to see Bogotá again...

HIS EXCELLENCY: Come on, Ihuou. Dogo will always be by your side. His bulk alone will make those zombies with four eyes to pee on the spot! [*laughs freely*]. Just think of the wonderful time on those fairy islands on the way to Bogotá. [*picks up the* YESSAH *papers*] By the way, we can't spend the whole day in sally gardens. Here...have this.

MARIAMA: [*snappy*] What's it? No more typing for today...I have hurt my finger and broken my nail.

HIS EXCELLENCY: Oh, not whitlows this time? ... Really, I can't say what's wrong with the intellectuals in this Kingdom, Maria. That clown, Nicodemus Yessah thinks he can use this as bribe to become one of my ministers.

MARIAMA: I'm not interested in your petty gossips, *Oga*... What is the next command, civilian General Napoleon Bonaparte?

HIS EXCELLENCY: Oh! ... Well, top-secret a copy to that bastard Amin. And then...

MARIAMA: [*biting*] No more orders for today, Black Napoleon ... [*snatches the papers and swing-walks away*]

HIS EXCELLENCY: Don't be so aggressive my dear; your foolish whitlows may explode like little grenades.

MARIAMA: I wish they'd explode into your hypnotized eyes. [*laughing, slams the door behind her*]

HIS EXCELLENCY: Oh! My beautiful bitch... you make me hungry for Bogotá too soon and forever!

<u>Scene II</u>

[*Evening:* CHINWAZU NWAPA's *study.* BENYALA BA *is alone in the room, humming. The door opens and* CHINWAZU *comes in with mastered dignity*]

BA: [*stops humming*] Any trace of him?

NWAPA: He is on his way. I called when he'd just left. [*sits down*] I'm really worried about his attitude Ba ...

BA: So you've noticed it at last?

NWAPA: What do you mean?

BA: I've learned to hold my tongue ... and the others too, it seems. The child who cries too much will never be taken seriously on the night of its death.

NWAPA: Okay, I'll tackle him immediately he comes in.

BA: [*comically*] What do you mean?

NWAPA: Tell him straight that he doesn't deserve the trust of the group any more.

BA: To my mind that'll be a hasty and risky step. What if there's nothing to tackle about him after all? I mean, what if it's only our imagination running wild. It can happen, you know. On the other hand and granted he has indeed eaten *soya* it will be unwise for us to confront him without concrete evidence of his own guilt. He'll either refuse or walk out and damn the consequences.

NWAPA: So what do you suggest?

BA: We simply play fox with him. When he comes in you'll ask at some point if anyone feels uncomfortable and will want to back out before we do the home run, as Americans will put it...

NWAPA: That'll still be betraying so much especially if he's guilty. What I think we should do is alter the time of the meeting.

BA: You're crazy, *Mister*!

NWAPA: I'm not. Many of us think we know His Excellency, but still take him for granted each time he appears to be cornered. The man is a perfect political chameleon, and who can blame him, when everyone seems to give in to what the poet has referred to as *climates of colossal gullibility*? But he is so simply because he can be nothing else; it is his nature. And to be a leader, any leader, you must have a grain of manipulative dictatorship in you, else ...

BA: Every sheep will rival him, and that's his greatest fear, right?

NWAPA: Perfect! I didn't know you were aware of my last publication, I mean in such detain.

BA: Well, let's say I had to do some background check on the state of your brains before committing myself to the cause.

NWAPA: Oho, so I wasn't alone! [*they laugh*] Mutual suspicion then ... but for a good cause, I hope. [*reflective*] But the worst thing with attempting to tackle a politician like His Excellency on his own spy-infested turf is to forget that he's the most mutating post-independence mystery both as a person and an ideology.

BA: Okay, I begin to get it, but how then for God's sake do we handle the diplomats and the press, tell me!

NWAPA: Okay, listen Ba. We may be wrong in our suppositions but we must act as if we're right. The original schedule is for 5pm. We take it back by three hours. That's the difference between Greenwich Mean Time and Black Man's Time: the one is formally fixed while the latter is always shivering on the whims of individual contingencies.

BA: What about Bob Dinard? If our fears are legitimate he may still Judas us.

NWAPA: I no longer understand Judas' alleged crime. But in that case, if we're pushed to the wall, we leave him out. When he comes in now we'll make our briefing as brief as possible. Then we part for you to come back here. We'll then contact the others and spend the whole night on the phone and coffee. I'm confident the diplomats and the foreign press will co-operate.

BA: Okay Sir. I'm converted. I needed just convincing.

[*somewhere in the house a bell rings*]

NWAPA: That must be Nicodemus – at the gate. Let's do something now. Even a child will know we were conspiring. Can we have a look at those posters now?

BA: [*untying them*] Sure boss.

[*a rap on the door, YESSAH breezes in*]

YESSAH: Oh boy, the place is deserted. Where the others?

NWAPA: You took your time, Nick.

23

YESSAH: The damn evening traffic in this forsaken city! But better late than never.

BA: Better never than *always* late Nico... I'll say that for you. You're always late for everything except your bite. [*laughs happily*]

YESSAH: Okay. Let's work now that I'm here. Any agenda?

NWAPA: Who should draw the agenda for us, Nick?

YESSAH: You're accusing me still! But you know I couldn't attend the mid-day session and can't dream of an agenda now that I don't know what was discussed. This damn mother-in-law of mine with her rotten kidney, you must understand my situation... What do you have there Ba? [*unfolds the poster*] Jesus wept! Do we really need all this literature, dears?

BA: Why not? Before you came in the boss was cursing me that they are not enough. I always receive knocks meant for you, Nick.

YESSAH: Thank God for you, Koffi. [*to* NWAPA] But you see Chinwa, we'll simply crowd the whole place with all this stuff and people are too soon bored with too much of literature; they prefer something graphic ... Let me see [*reads*] **THE MAN DIES IN ALL WHO KEEP SILENT IN THE FACE OF TYRANNY... THOSE WHO MAKE PEACEFUL CHANGE IMPOSSIBLE, MAKE VIOLENT CHANGE INEVITABLE ... THE FIRST STEP TOWARD THE DETHRONEMENT OF TERROR IS THE DEFLATION OF ITS HYPOCRITICAL SELF-RIGHTEOUSNESS ...**[*to* NWAPA] Can't we make do with these, Chinwa? We only need to make the print bolder.

NWAPA: Of course we can; but I'm afraid they won't tell the whole story. Take the poetic excerpts for instance. Just listen... [*reads*] **ALIEN MINDS MUST LEARN RECUMBENT POSTURES ... MY NAME IS THE KEY TO DREAMS ... IN CLIMATES OF COLOSSAL GULLIBILITY SHROUDING OVER ANY OTHER CATECHISM, LORD GRANT THAT WE PROTECT THE DREAMER & THE POET ... IF YOU WANT TO KNOW THE SEX OF LAGOONS JUMP, JUMP INTO THEIR WOMBS...**

YESSAH: Okay, Chinwa, I give in. You always win. [*laughs dryly*]

NWAPA: Thank you. We delayed diner for you.

YESSAH: Good boy! I have wolves in my bowels, gentlemen. We can work all night thereafter.

BA: Just like you, Nick...

NWAPA: Let's go.

Scene III

[*The following day – 3.30pm. The auditorium of St. John's Center. The animated conversation of the audience dies down as* CHINWAZU NWAPA *takes the floor. As he talks, there are sporadic shouts of 'Fire!' and 'Hear!' and 'man no run!' from the audience*]

NWAPA: Your Excellencies, Honorable members of the diplomatic corps, ladies and gentlemen, we're indeed grateful for your understanding over the last minute hitches that necessitated the change of venue. Without much delay and given the gravity of the situation, I wish to let you know that we're at a crisis moment in Nubialand. We're also risking a visit from the Gestapo of State any moment this afternoon and greatly appreciate your decision to be part of any eventuality. That's proof of the urgent necessity to find enduring solutions in our common struggle. The launching of Professor Nso'ika Mazuwiy's multi-dimensional book, *The Archetypal Nubialand Intellectual and the Diasporic Mirage*, with its telling sub-title, *Neoliberal Romance with Three-Piece Gunocrats*, is a monumental event which provides the platform for us to discuss certain issues which are vital to the statehood of Nubialand. I'll introduce our areas of concern and then the Group will entertain the relevant questions... [*sips from his glass*] As I talk to you now, ladies and gentlemen, the legendary dignity of Nubialand is very much in question. The notion of Negroid existentialism, that is, the potential in this species to be subjected without complaint to all forms of frustration and humiliation, has baffled even the most ardent exponents of Basque-Nazi Ku-Klux Klanism together with the pious faithfuls of a Jobbian eternity. This can be demonstrated by the single fact that the very archetype of our struggle, the eminent Professor Mongo Wa Swolenka, is a destitute to foreign charity thousands of kilometres from home. This is our main concern in organizing this meeting. We're committed to stand by him and campaign for his return and will not retreat, never, even at the point of the bayonet ... Our second point concerns our most prestigious award, the Dynamite Prize. We are worried about the end of such recognition when, as in the case of Nubialand, the recognized person ends up as the fugitive of society. One variable of development and underdevelopment is the manner in which the respective societies treat their artists. Where tyranny blooms, the artist is often behind bars, branded as public enemy number one. So we question the Prize because the intentions behind it are compromised by its inability to rid the instinct of stagnating violence from human consciousness, a significant and sad reminder of its parentage, and in fact explains the criminally bloody fate of Nubialand. Born of war profiteering as we all wish to forget today, such an award makes us guilty accomplices in the potential death of our land, if we choose to remain silent in the face of tyranny as shiploads of mines, bombs and guns are daily shored into the Kingdom. Apart from this conspiracy of armed capitalism that breeds eternal despots, the very humiliation heaped on Professor Swolenka defines the state of Democracy and freedom in Nubialand. The ideal of Democracy has been shackled wherever it manifests in the land. Take for instance the local bye-elections in the twin States of Akwachaland and Bassa. But here, let the example of Soweto village teach us. The villagers drove away Anglo-American corporations as a protest for their Chief to give everyone of them the individual right to choose their representatives in the Provincial Assembly. The whole of Nubialand can learn from Soweto how to endure suffering and succeed in the end by overthrowing this successive gang of junta regimes in the land. This will only be possible when we remember what the bed bug told her panicking children, when their home was on fire: everything that is hot eventually cools down. This will also be possible when the language of international diplomacy is changed and the international community recognises not Governments that may be legal without being legitimate, but States and Peoples who are the legitimate custodians of every Government. Until Government becomes the instrument of the People, beholden to it, the very People remain a toy in an authoritarian nightmare ...

[*Sudden screeching of tyres outside; there is a general stampede as feet run along the corridors amidst a confused harmony of whistles. In the confusion,* NWAPA *repeatedly shouts* 'BE CALM LADIES AND GENTLEMEN!' ... 'THIS IS THE HOUR OF OUR PASSION ... BE PATIENT!' *Then suddenly the imposing image of* AMIN *blocks the doorway*]

AMIN: [*snarling*] In the name of His Most Royal Excellency Bob Gbadarango Binyambutu Buthablaizi, aka BGB[2], Supreme Commander of the Nubialand Armed Forces and Benevolent Defender of the People's Revolution, and by the Constitution of his immortal dream, which he vows to defend eternally, etcetera, etcetera, I condemn all of you for hatching subversive designs against the integrity of the Kingdom...

NWAPA: For shame, Colonel Amin, for national shame, for international dignity!

AMIN: [*with blind enthusiasm*] Who says? Shame is human sentiment that devalues the national purse. Anyway, from here all the diplomatic spies drive straight to the Headquarters of the Supreme Military Council. You'll be honoured with a military escort.

NWAPA: Excuse Mr. Colonel, this is an authorized meeting and you have no right to disrupt it!

AMIN: Who issued the authorization for this hour and venue, you Professor of lies? See how even your big book can't save you from your own trap?

NWAPA: [*faces AMIN squarely*] Are you so shamelessly crazy, Mister Colonel? Must you confess so much of your bloody guilt, inadequacy, and vandalism?

[*an OFFICER hurries in and stiffens to attention*]

OFFICER: [*to AMIN*] A man ahside Sah. Say he is VIP

AMIN: [*suspicious*] How? Who is it? Bring him in.

OFFICER: Yes Sah! [*stands aside and YESSAH comes in*]

YESSAH: [*to NWAPA and AMIN*] What accursed trick have you played on me? I demand an explanation!

AMIN: [*seizes YESSAH by the throat*] In whose government, you goat? You bungled up the schedule so as to ridicule His Excellency. And now you demand an explanation. [*shoves him away*] Traitor!!

NWAPA and BA: Nicodemus!!

YESSAH: [*rubbing his neck*] There's been a disastrous mix-up somewhere... I'm not to blame. The kiss of Judas was never of betrayal but of fulfilment, so don't stare at me like that!

AMIN: His Excellency will thank you for that. This is a divine Gunocracy, Professor, where expediency is the password ... a system where weak civilians and their weakened form of ballot leadership either lean on the barrel of the gun or are catapulted out of existence by the venom of the pistol. But we also metamorphose, and dump the khaki for the sheep skin of democracy. [OFFICER *approaches him and they confide*]

BA: What really happened, Nicodemus?

YESSAH: [*defiant*] Indeed, what really happened! I knew all along that you people were erecting my cross behind my back.

NWAPA: Simply because you rehearsed the Judas-kiss every time you gave us a slip... Shame on you, Nicodemus!

YESSAH: For what? There's nothing whatsoever to be ashamed of. If you want to know I simply weighed my priorities from a perceptive dimension like any sane and courageous man should.

NWAPA: I never really believe you were such a mean beetle, Nicodemus. Now I hate you.

YESSAH: Do as you wish. At least you've learned something new today. One's life is one's cross and one doesn't need so much advice on how to carry it even if it breaks one's neck.

AMIN: [*nodding* OFFICER *away; to* YESSAH] Enough traitor! His Excellency never forgives traitors who can't deliver on the simplest of assignments. [*calls out*] Dogo!

OFFICER: [*off-stage*] Mon Co-o-nel!! [*appears at the door*]

AMIN: [*indicates* YESSAH] Pack this traitorous garbage away. You know how to entertain him.

DOGO: [*grinning*] Yes, Mon Co-o-nel. Professor, *oya* ... [*drags* YESSAH *out*]

AMIN: [*to* NWAPA *and* BA] Now, gentlemen, can we too cue in from where we left off? No complications so far.

NWAPA: Listen Colonel Amin. We have planned this out carefully and will go on, Yessahs or no Yessahs. Now, go and tell your master that we will never surrender even at the point of the bayonet...go!

AMIN: Is that so? Then I'll start with you, *okro*-soup head... Dogo! bring in the chains, fast!!

[*there is a scuffle between them, drowned by the sound of exploding tear gas; then a general stampede and sustained whistling. Black-out*]

Scene IV

[N*ight,* HIS EXCELLENCY'*s office. He is pacing the room, tense; he should gulp whisky and smoke profusely at close intervals. From time to time the sound of splashing water, whipping or screaming, breaks in from the adjoining room.* MARIAMA, *dressed in a flowery bikini, is perched at the end of the table watching* HIS EXCELLENCY'*s movements*]

HIS EXCELLENCY: [*to no one in particular*] They have bungled up everything! This was supposed to be a clean-up job with no smears. But now I can't really justify myself. [*to* MARIAMA *who is unmoved*] Gunocracy needs concrete and precise justifications Mariama ... Gunocracy is my special science, the key to future leadership against neoliberal snares; but now pumpkin heads have bungled up everything [*walks toward the torture chamber and viciously kicks the door open. His tone trembles with a sadist's mirth*] Dogo, bring out the ape. [DOGO *drags out* YESSAH *dripping and staggering;* HIS EXCELLENCY *boots him to the floor*]

YESSAH: Have mercy!

HIS EXCELLENCY: The mercy of Gunocrats is to eliminate the object of mercy, Professor Yessah. I tolerate no blunders; otherwise, you'll have to wait for the Second Coming, whenever.

YESSAH: This is foul play, Your Excellency, hitting your own man beneath the belt without pity!

HIS EXCELLENCY: Who draws the rules, Yessah? Am I not privileged to shift the goalpost as often as I see fit for the evolution of the game, that is, twist the law without breaking it?

YESSAH: But you said sir, that scratch my back I scratch your back: that's what you said in the beginning of our understanding, and I believed you in the fair spirit of comradeship.

HIS EXCELLENCY: You're a capital fool then, Professor Yessah. When shall you or anyone in this Kingdom ever learn that the politics of back-scratching always ends with back-stabbing? In fact, the original creed is, scratch my back I stab your back, and I call that fair play. Is it my fault that one mighty head can be more than the seventeen million in your petering constituency, which I drug religiously with polluted milk from comrade Moa Chin? Come to think of it, desperation is making the world crowd at my knee, for a piece of my timber from the enclaves of Yokodoma. Who will deprive me of my due, when my benevolence helps to stem the spectre of global warming, care of Detroit furnaces? You're a big fool Yessah, and I don't like fools. [*To guard*] Take him away.

YESSAH: But hear me out, my lord, alpha omega of Nubian universe, hear me out. A lot may dangle on my word!

HIS EXCELLENCY: [*holds up his hand*] What now?

YESSAH: The small print, Sir, below the contractual statement of intent, which I proposed, the key to your administrative and intelligence vision. No one will notice it when your invisible hand sweeps criminal minds into the bunker.

HIS EXCELLENCY: [*flips through the folder on his table and fishes out a paper; puts on his glasses and peers at the paper, reads*] 'His Excellency's Number One Secretary of State for Ideas and Ideological Surveillance'. [*looks up, a nasty grimace on his face*] Wha's this, Professor Yessah? Teacher teach me

34

no nonsense, understand? Such useless clowns, the burden of my leadership! In any case, I'll edit your wish to read *Agency for Idiotic Membranes*. Take him away, *akung*!

YESSAH: You mean Sir…

HIS EXCELLENCY: I mean nothing, Yessah. Read my lips, if you don't have ears. The oracle speaks only once and those with ears are not many these days. Read my lips, Yessah [*makes an obscene sign*] … see? At times silence is divine, and I'm no stranger to the machinations of clowns like you eyeing my throne. Fellows like you are a nuisance to civilized leadership which I represent, and how would humanity fare, tell me, in the excesses of your blunders and God knows what else! You keep making excuses my dear sir, to hide your own inadequacies. [*mimics*] If I were rich I'd build the whole world and ensure eternal life for all humanity … my leader cripples all my effort … and my family starves from destitution … [*in his normal voice*] … and so much more, Yessah. But what did your lot do in the days of plenty? If a man can't save a franc when he earns a thousand a week, then he'll never save a franc if I pay him a million a day. Your own ruinous ways are your crucifix and I refuse to be your legendary scapegoat anymore!

YESSAH: But only one head has the privilege to wear the crown at any given moment, my lord.

HIS EXCELLENCY: Hypocrite! You wish to pretend foresight and flatter me into unguarded concessions, eh! Or that it may soon be your turn or someone else's? But what have I not done for you and your lot, and what is the result? Barren intellectualism, year in year out, licking my boots and prostrating like beggars, with nothing to show except half cooked pages of dreadful, outdated research? What have I not done in my endless benevolence that any messiah would?

YESSAH: My latest volume, Sir, about to come out of the press, and I was counting on your usual patronage to ... you know! Every gold medal belongs to your Excellency, and we're mere messengers of your glory.

HIS EXCELLENCY: [*reflecting*] As if I've not done more than enough. As if my effort to campaign for Nubian Day of Warlessness is a minor task. I need my accolades, yes, but not after my head would have been hewn off my shoulder. Every neck bears only one head, my dear sir!

YESSAH: Still I hear and know things, Your Royal Excellency...

HIS EXCELLENCY: No, Yessah ... you have already earned your privileges. Now you must go out the way I brought you in ... through the window. Fortunately you are a theatre man, always on stage, even now as you lick your wounds... Bye-bye Nicodemus ... Dogo!

[DOGO *drags him howling and face-backward back into the torture room.* HIS EXCELLENCY *turns round sharply as* AMIN *comes in*]

HIS EXCELLENCY: What now, you crippled brain?

AMIN: Some success, Your Excellency! One of the three runaways already apprehended!

HIS EXCELLENCY: It changes nothing, Amin. I didn't order for bloodshed ... not for this operation, and the most important assignment of your career. Look at the balance sheet: a member of the group murdered in cold blood, two of their leaders are at large...

AMIN: But we have the real leader, Your Excellency!

HIS EXCELLENCY: What of it? You think Professor Chinwazu Nwapa is disappointed? His dream has always been to be a very important prisoner and you have so stupidly served his purpose. All he now awaits is the international publicity which is sure to come, not to talk of the fact that millions of dollars will be wasted on his fat jowls to allay the wrath of his foreign conspirators. You have propped him up the throne of living martyrdom. [*almost tearful*] Why have you crippled my vision, Badamasi, why? Get out of my sight you wretch!

[AMIN *rushes out of the room;* HIS EXCELLENCY *stares ahead, as if hypnotized. The moment is sustained, then* MARIAMA, *breaking from her apparent cramp, walks up to him and steers him gently to his chair*]

MARIAMA: Now, you need rest, real rest, dear. You've been cracking your brains for nothing.

HIS EXCELLENCY: For nothing, Mariama?

MARIAMA: Of course! Nobody in the whole Kingdom deserves you. [HIS EXCELLENCY's *countenance relaxes a bit*] Look, my Excellency, I alone know your worth, and that is everything.

HIS EXCELLENCY: Come on, Mariama, how excellent am I in essence with such banalities as I now exhibit?

MARIAMA: You begin to rant again! Forget this quest for ideals. You can find none beyond yourself and that's all you need. Leave all behind, dear; abandon everything and simply take me to Bogota. You have a fortune abroad and with me...

HIS EXCELLENCY: Never! I say never! [*pushes MARIAMA off his knees and stands up and talks abstractly*] I started this, I must see it through. I still hold the reins of power in the palm of my hands and no one is going to stop me!! You just wait an see how I dazzle humanity, I, the Alpha and Omega in contemporary leadership, if you know what I mean, the sword of Longinus in my fist, yes, and I wield it like the hero of my heart with no straw brains to obstruct my way because as it was in the beginning of my incarnation, is now more than ever before, and shall forever and ever, ever be, the plenitude of my enigmatic brains substituting God in the vicinity of deprived and dispossessed mankind, and who cares in the end, who cares, eh, who, Mariama if the ablution of my eternity requires the blood of a sacrificial lamb with varsity credentials ...

[*as he walks briskly toward the torture room from where the sound of YESSAH's screams rises anew, and MARIAMA stares helplessly after him, lights fade and go out*]

CURTAINS.